POLICE TV

How much money do you take with you when you go shopping? Are you careful? Sometimes people steal money in the street – then you need the police to help you.

Dan, Sue, and Jim are police officers in London. They are not happy because a robber steals money from people near some shops every day.

How can they find the robber? What does the robber look like – is it a man or a woman? Old or young? It is not always easy to know.

What do they have to help them? They have radios – but robbers have phones. Dan, Sue, and Jim need something that the robber doesn't have – they need Police TV!

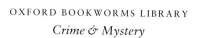

OXFORD BOOKWORMS LIBRARY
Crime & Mystery

Police TV

Starter (250 headwords)

TIM VICARY

Police TV

Illustrated by
Dylan Teague

OXFORD UNIVERSITY PRESS

OXFORD
UNIVERSITY PRESS

Great Clarendon Street, Oxford OX2 6DP

Oxford University Press is a department of the University of Oxford.
It furthers the University's objective of excellence in research, scholarship,
and education by publishing worldwide in

Oxford New York

Auckland Cape Town Dar es Salaam Hong Kong Karachi
Kuala Lumpur Madrid Melbourne Mexico City Nairobi
New Delhi Shanghai Taipei Toronto

With offices in

Argentina Austria Brazil Chile Czech Republic France Greece
Guatemala Hungary Italy Japan Poland Portugal Singapore
South Korea Switzerland Thailand Turkey Ukraine Vietnam

OXFORD and OXFORD ENGLISH are registered trade marks of
Oxford University Press in the UK and in certain other countries

This edition © Oxford University Press 2008

The moral rights of the author have been asserted

Database right Oxford University Press (maker)

First published in Oxford Bookworms 2000

8 10 9

ISBN: 978 0 19 423425 2

A complete recording of this Bookworms edition of
Police TV is available on audio CD. ISBN 978 0 19 423407 8

Printed in China

Word count (main text): 1530

For more information on the Oxford Bookworms Library, visit
www.oup.com/bookworms

This book is printed on paper from certified and well-managed sources.

CONTENTS

1 THE JOGGER

Dan and Sue are police officers in London. It is a Tuesday morning, and Dan is angry.

'What's the matter, Dan?' Sue asks.

'Look at this,' Dan says. 'Every day someone steals money from people near the shops. We must stop this.'

'Yes, of course,' Sue says. 'But who is it?'

'There is a jogger,' Dan says. 'Every day he runs near the shops. Sometimes he runs into people. Perhaps he steals the money.'

'OK,' Sue says. 'Let's go to the shops. Perhaps we can see this jogger.'

They sit upstairs in a window over the shops. Dan has a radio. They watch the people in the street.

'Look!' Sue says. 'There's the jogger!'

The young man runs into an old woman, and she falls down. The jogger puts his hand on the old woman's arm. 'I'm sorry,' he says. 'Can I help you? Here's your bag.'

Then a young woman shouts at him. 'Don't run here!' she says. 'It's dangerous! Go away!'

The young man runs away. Dan talks in his radio. 'Quick! Stop him! He's running up North Street!'

A police car stops the young man in North Street.

'Are you OK now?' Sue asks the old woman.

'Yes, thank you. Where is that nice young woman? I can't see her now.'

'Have you got all your money?' Sue asks.

The old woman looks in her bag. 'No, I haven't! My money's in my purse. But my purse isn't here!'

'OK Sue,' Dan says. 'Let's talk to the jogger!'

'Who are you?' Sue asks the young man.

'My name's Peter Jones. Why? Who are you?'

'We're police officers. Why do you go running past the shops every day?'

'Why not? I like running.'

'OK,' Dan says. 'Let's look for the money.'

'What money?' Peter Jones asks. 'What are you talking about? I never take money with me when I run.'

Dan looks for the money but he cannot find any.

'Can I go now?' Peter Jones asks.

'OK,' Dan says angrily. 'But don't come back!'

'Why not?' Peter asks angrily. 'I live here! And I'm not doing anything wrong!' He runs away.

'What do we do now?' Sue asks. 'Where is the old woman's money, and her purse?'

'I don't know,' says Dan. 'Somebody has it. But who?'

2 TV

Dan and Sue go back to the shops. 'I don't understand,' Dan says. 'The jogger hasn't got the money so we must look for someone different.'

'Look,' Sue says. 'There's a TV camera over that shop door. Perhaps that can help us.'

They go into the shop and watch the video.

'Look,' Sue says. 'There's the old woman. She's getting money from the bank and putting it into her purse. Now she's putting the purse into the bag.'

'Stop the video there,' says Dan. 'Now, look carefully. Is anybody watching her?'

'There are a lot of people in the street,' Sue says. 'I'm not sure. Is it that man with the long hair?'

'Perhaps,' says Dan. 'Let's go on. What happens next?'

They watch the video. The jogger runs into the old lady. He stops and helps her. She shouts at him and he runs away. Then a lot of people come and help the old lady.

'Look!' Sue says. 'The long-haired man has her arm.'

'Yes, but that woman has her bag,' Dan says. 'What's she doing with it? Oh! I can't see! There's a man in front of her!'

9

'Listen, I have an idea,' Dan says. 'You go to the bank tomorrow, and take some money out.'

'Why's that a good idea?' Sue asks.

'Because we can watch you,' Dan answers. 'Get a lot of money from the bank, and let everybody in the street see it. Take a radio too, so you can talk to me.'

'OK,' Sue says. 'We can do that tomorrow morning, then.'

❸ HELP ME! QUICK!

Next day Sue goes to the bank. Dan is watching with another policeman, Jim. They have radios.

'I'm getting the money now,' Sue says.

'That's good, Sue,' Dan says on his radio. 'Now let everybody see it.'

Sue drops some money near her feet. People in the street look at her.

'Look – there's the man with the long hair!' Jim says. 'He's picking up the money. Shall I arrest him?'

'No, wait,' Dan says. 'Watch.'

The man picks up the money and gives it to Sue. 'Here you are,' he says. 'That's a lot of money – be careful!'

'Thanks,' Sue says.

'That's OK.' The man smiles and walks away.

'Have you got all the money, Sue?' Dan asks by radio. 'Yes, it's all here,' Sue says. 'What can I do now?'

'Buy some things in the shops, and then walk slowly down the street,' Dan says. 'We're watching you.'

Sue buys some apples, milk and bread. Then she walks slowly down the street. Dan and Jim watch her go.

'Is anybody following me?' Sue asks.

'No,' Dan says. 'There's a woman with a baby. That's all.'

'Don't follow me,' Sue says into the radio. 'Nobody must see you. I'm turning right, into Smith Street . . . now I'm turning left into Peg Lane. The woman with the baby is following me . . . I'm turning right, into Dale Avenue.'

'Are there lots of people about?' Dan asks.

'No, it's very quiet. Nothing is happening.'

Dan and Jim wait. Then Sue shouts: 'Be careful! Oh, help me, quick! Help!'

The jogger, Peter Jones, runs into Sue and she falls over. There are apples, milk and bread everywhere.

'I'm sorry,' says the man. 'Let me help you.'

The woman takes Sue's arm. 'Are you OK?' she asks. 'Go away!' she shouts at the man.

But he sees the radio in Sue's pocket. 'What's this?' he asks. 'A police radio? Give me the money, quick!'

He takes the money and runs.

15

The woman wants to run after him but Sue holds her.
'Stop!' she says. 'I'm a police officer. You must stay here!'

'But why?' the woman asks. 'I want to help you. That
man has your money – I haven't got it!'

'Is he your friend?' Sue asks. 'Where does he live?'

'I don't know,' the woman says. 'I don't know him.'

'Who are you?' Sue asks. 'Where do you live?'

'Linda . . . Linda Wilks. I live at 14, Old Street.'

4 MAN WITH A KNIFE

Dan runs up to Sue. 'Are you OK?' he asks.

'Yes, I'm OK,' she says. 'Go on, Dan – run!'

Sue calls a police car on her radio. Dan runs after Peter Jones. 'Jim, he's turning left into Dock Lane!' he shouts. 'Can you see him?'

'I can see him but he's running very fast,' Jim says. The jogger sees Jim and gets into a boat. Jim runs to the river and gets into the boat, too.

'Stop!' Jim says. 'I'm a police officer – Oh no!'

The jogger, Peter Jones, hits Jim and he falls into the water. The boat goes across the river.

Dan helps Jim out of the water. 'He's going into a café,' Dan says. 'Come on – let's run to that bridge!'

They go across the bridge and run to the café. Jim goes behind the café and Dan goes in.

'Is he in there?' Jim asks on his radio.

'Yes,' Dan answers. 'Jim – he's coming out!'

'Stop,' says Jim. 'I'm a police officer.'

But Peter has a knife in his hand.

Jim holds out his hand. 'Give me the knife, Peter.'

'Stay back!' Peter says. 'I can kill you with this.'

Jim can see Dan in the door behind Peter. Dan walks out of the door, very slowly and quietly.

'Come on, Peter,' says Jim. 'Give me the knife.'

Dan takes Peter's arms from behind, and Jim takes the knife from his hand. Dan finds the money in Peter's trousers.

5 AT THE POLICE STATION

'I want to go home now,' says Linda. 'My baby is hungry and tired.'

'Do you know Peter Jones?' Sue asks. 'Do you and Peter steal money from people?'

'No, I don't know him. And I never steal money.'

'Do you know this woman, Peter?' Dan asks.

'No,' says Peter. 'I don't know her. Who is she?'

Dan and Sue go back to their office.

'Does Linda work with Peter?' Dan asks Sue.

'Yes, she does,' says Sue. 'Watch this video. Look – there she is! She's watching me get the money, and now she's talking to someone on her phone.'

'But who is she talking to?'

'She's talking to Peter, of course. Now she's following me and talking to him again. She's talking about me.'

Dan and Sue speak to Linda again.

'Can I see your phone, please, Ms Wilks?' Sue asks.

'My phone? Why do you want to see that?'

'Well, it remembers a lot of numbers.'

Sue presses *1* on Linda's phone. Peter's phone begins to ring. Sue laughs. 'Let me ask you again, Ms Wilks. Do you know Peter Jones?'

'Well, yes, OK. I know him. But I don't steal money.'

Sue and Dan take Linda home. They go into her house.

'There's two hundred pounds under your bed, Linda,' Dan says. 'And look – this is the old lady's purse.'

'This is a nice photo of you and the baby,' Sue says. 'But who is the man? Is he the baby's father?'

'OK, it's Peter,' says Linda. 'And yes, I do steal the money. I'm sorry, OK?'

'No, Linda, it's not OK,' Sue says. 'It's not OK at all.'

GLOSSARY

arrest (*vb*) when the police find a bad man and take him to
  the police station
bridge a road or path that goes over water
buy get something from a shop with money
café a place where you sit and drink coffee or tea
dangerous something that can hurt you is dangerous
follow walk behind someone
idea something you think
jogger a runner
let make it easy for something to happen
officer a man or woman in the police
purse a small bag for money
shout talk very loudly
steal take something that is not yours
turn go left or right

Police TV

ACTIVITIES

Before Reading

1 Look at the front and back covers and then answer the questions. Tick one box for each question.

1 When does the story happen?

   a ☐ In the present.

   b ☐ In the future.

   c ☐ Long ago.

2 Who is the story about?

   a ☐ Young people.

   b ☐ Older people.

   c ☐ Children.

3 Who steals money from people?

   a ☐ Dan.

   b ☐ A robber.

   c ☐ The police.

4 What kind of story is this?

   a ☐ Frightening.

   b ☐ Exciting.

   c ☐ ……… (You can write your own answer.)

While Reading

1 Read pages 1–3 and then answer these questions.

1 What happens every day near the shops?
   a ☐ A woman likes running there.
   b ☐ Someone takes money from people.
   c ☐ Dan and Sue go shopping.

2 What does the young man do to the old woman?
   a ☐ He puts his hand on her arm.
   b ☐ He puts his hand on her leg.
   c ☐ He takes her bag.

2 Read pages 4–6. Who says this in the story?

1 'Have you got all your money?'
2 'My purse isn't here!
3 'I like running.'
4 'OK. But don't come back!'

3 Read Chapter 2. Answer these questions.

1 What does Sue see over the shop door?
2 What do Dan and Sue do in the shop?
3 How many people come to help the old lady?
4 Who goes to the bank and takes some money out?

4 Read Chapter 3.
Are these statements true (T) or false (F)?

	T	F
1 The man with the long hair picks up the money.	☐	☐
2 The man with the long hair takes the money from Sue.	☐	☐
3 Sue is following a woman with a baby.	☐	☐
4 It's very quiet in Dale Avenue.	☐	☐
5 Peter Jones takes the radio from Sue's pocket.	☐	☐

5 Read Chapter 4. Answer these questions.

Who

1 . . . calls a police car on her radio?
2 . . . hits Jim?
3 . . . helps Jim out of the water?
4 . . . goes behind the cafe?
5 . . . takes Peter's arms from behind?

6 Before you read Chapter 5,
can you guess what happens?

	YES	NO
1 The police take Peter to the police station.	☐	☐
2 Linda knows Peter.	☐	☐
3 Linda tries to help Peter.	☐	☐
4 Linda is angry with Peter.	☐	☐
5 Peter runs away, but Linda finds him.	☐	☐

ACTIVITIES

After Reading

1 Use these words to join these sentences together.

and   but   so   because

1 Peter Jones runs into the old woman. She falls down.
2 The old woman looks in her bag. She can't find her purse.
3 Dan has a radio. He can talk to Sue.
4 Peter is afraid. He sees a radio in Sue's pocket.

2 Put these seven sentences in the right order.

a ☐ Peter Jones runs into Sue.
b ☐ She drops the money in the street.
c ☐ Sue walks into Smith Street, Peg Lane, and Dale Avenue.
d ☐ He sees the radio in her pocket, takes her money, and runs.
e ☐ The blue-haired man picks up the money and gives it to her.
f ☐ The woman with the baby follows her.
g ☐ Sue takes some money out of the bank.

3 **Look at each picture, then answer the questions after it.**

1
Who is this?
What is she doing?

2
Who is this?
What is she doing?

3
Who is this?
What is she doing?

4
Who is this?
Who is she talking to?

5
Who is this?
What is he doing?

6
Who is this?
What is he doing?

ABOUT THE AUTHOR

Tim Vicary is an experienced teacher and writer. He has written many stories for the Oxford Bookworms Library. These include *White Death* (Stage 1, Thriller & Adventure) and *The Elephant Man* (Stage 1, True Stories). He has two children, and keeps dogs, cats, and horses. He lives and works in York, in the north of England. He has published two long novels, *The Blood upon the Rose* and *Cat and Mouse*.

OXFORD BOOKWORMS LIBRARY

*Classics • Crime & Mystery • Factfiles • Fantasy & Horror
Human Interest • Playscripts • Thriller & Adventure
True Stories • World Stories*

The OXFORD BOOKWORMS LIBRARY provides enjoyable reading in English, with a wide range of classic and modern fiction, non-fiction, and plays. It includes original and adapted texts in seven carefully graded language stages, which take learners from beginner to advanced level. An overview is given on the next pages.

All Stage 1 titles are available as audio recordings, as well as over eighty other titles from Starter to Stage 6. All Starters and many titles at Stages 1 to 4 are specially recommended for younger learners. Every Bookworm is illustrated, and Starters and Factfiles have full-colour illustrations.

The OXFORD BOOKWORMS LIBRARY also offers extensive support. Each book contains an introduction to the story, notes about the author, a glossary, and activities. Additional resources include tests and worksheets, and answers for these and for the activities in the books. There is advice on running a class library, using audio recordings, and the many ways of using Oxford Bookworms in reading programmes. Resource materials are available on the website <www.oup.com/bookworms>.

The *Oxford Bookworms Collection* is a series for advanced learners. It consists of volumes of short stories by well-known authors, both classic and modern. Texts are not abridged or adapted in any way, but carefully selected to be accessible to the advanced student.

You can find details and a full list of titles in the *Oxford Bookworms Library Catalogue* and *Oxford English Language Teaching Catalogues*, and on the website <www.oup.com/bookworms>.

THE OXFORD BOOKWORMS LIBRARY
GRADING AND SAMPLE EXTRACTS

STARTER • 250 HEADWORDS

present simple – present continuous – imperative –
can/cannot, must – *going to* (future) – simple gerunds …

Her phone is ringing – but where is it?

Sally gets out of bed and looks in her bag. No phone. She looks under the bed. No phone. Then she looks behind the door. There is her phone. Sally picks up her phone and answers it. ***Sally's Phone***

STAGE I • 400 HEADWORDS

… past simple – coordination with *and*, *but*, *or* –
subordination with *before*, *after*, *when*, *because*, *so* …

I knew him in Persia. He was a famous builder and I worked with him there. For a time I was his friend, but not for long. When he came to Paris, I came after him – I wanted to watch him. He was a very clever, very dangerous man. ***The Phantom of the Opera***

STAGE 2 • 700 HEADWORDS

… present perfect – *will* (future) – *(don't) have to*, *must not*, *could* –
comparison of adjectives – simple *if* clauses – past continuous –
tag questions – *ask/tell* + infinitive …

While I was writing these words in my diary, I decided what to do. I must try to escape. I shall try to get down the wall outside. The window is high above the ground, but I have to try. I shall take some of the gold with me – if I escape, perhaps it will be helpful later. ***Dracula***

... should, may – present perfect continuous – *used to* – past perfect –
causative – relative clauses – indirect statements ...

Of course, it was most important that no one should see
Colin, Mary, or Dickon entering the secret garden. So Colin
gave orders to the gardeners that they must all keep away
from that part of the garden in future. ***The Secret Garden***

STAGE 4 • 1400 HEADWORDS

... past perfect continuous – passive (simple forms) –
would conditional clauses – indirect questions –
relatives with *where/when* – gerunds after prepositions/phrases ...

I was glad. Now Hyde could not show his face to the world
again. If he did, every honest man in London would be proud
to report him to the police. ***Dr Jekyll and Mr Hyde***

STAGE 5 • 1800 HEADWORDS

... future continuous – future perfect –
passive (modals, continuous forms) –
would have conditional clauses – modals + perfect infinitive ...

If he had spoken Estella's name, I would have hit him. I was so
angry with him, and so depressed about my future, that I could
not eat the breakfast. Instead I went straight to the old house.
Great Expectations

STAGE 6 • 2500 HEADWORDS

... passive (infinitives, gerunds) – advanced modal meanings –
clauses of concession, condition

When I stepped up to the piano, I was confident. It was as if I
knew that the prodigy side of me really did exist. And when I
started to play, I was so caught up in how lovely I looked that
I didn't worry how I would sound. ***The Joy Luck Club***

BOOKWORMS · CRIME & MYSTERY · STARTER

Girl on a Motorcycle

JOHN ESCOTT

'Give me the money,' says the robber to the Los Angeles security guard. The guard looks at the gun and hands over the money. The robber has long blond hair and rides a motorcycle – and a girl with long blond hair arrives at Kenny's motel – on a motorcycle. Is she the robber?

BOOKWORMS · CRIME & MYSTERY · STARTER

Give us the Money

MAEVE CLARKE

'Every day is the same. Nothing exciting ever happens to me,' thinks Adam one boring Monday morning. But today is not the same. When he helps a beautiful young woman because some men want to take her bag, life gets exciting and very, very dangerous.

New York Café
MICHAEL DEAN

It is the year 2030, and an e-mail message arrives at New York Café: 'I want to help people and make them happy!' But not everybody is happy about the e-mail, and soon the police and the President are very interested in the New York Café.

Survive!
HELEN BROOKE

You are in a small plane, going across the Rocky Mountains. Suddenly, the engine starts to make strange noises . . .

Soon you are alone, in the snow, at the top of a mountain, and it is very, very cold. Can you find your way out of the mountain?

BOOKWORMS · TRUE STORIES · STAGE 1

The Elephant Man

TIM VICARY

He is not beautiful. His mother does not want him, and children run away from him. People laugh at him, and call him 'The Elephant Man'.

Then someone speaks to him – and listens to him! At the age of twenty-seven, Joseph Merrick finds a friend for the first time in his life.

This is a true and tragic story. It is also a famous film.

BOOKWORMS · THRILLER & ADVENTURE · STAGE 1

White Death

TIM VICARY

Sarah Harland is nineteen, and she is in prison. At the airport, they find heroin in her bag. So, now she is waiting to go to court. If the court decides that it was her heroin, then she must die.

She says she did not do it. But if she did not, who did? Only two people can help Sarah: her mother, and an old boyfriend who does not love her now. Can they work together? Can they find the real criminal before it is too late?